The Last Day Before Exile

Published by 404 Ink Limited
www.404Ink.com
@404Ink

Please note: Some references include URLs which may change or be unavailable
after publication of this book. All references within endnotes were accessible
and accurate as of October 2023 but may experience link rot from there on in.

Editing: Laura Jones-Rivera
Typesetting: Laura Jones-Rivera
Proofreading: Laura Jones-Rivera
Cover design: Luke Bird
Co-founders and publishers of 404 Ink:
Heather McDaid & Laura Jones-Rivera

Print ISBN: 978-1-912489-80-0
Ebook ISBN: 978-1-912489-81-7

Printed and bound in Great Britain by Clays Ltd, Elcograf S.p.A.

The Last Day Before Exile

Stories of Resistance, Displacement & Finding Home

Selin Bucak

Inklings

Contents

Introduction   I

Chapter 1
Can you feel at home in a foreign country?   9

Chapter 2
Those who didn't know   31

Chapter 3
A state of terror and confusion   53

Chapter 4
Waiting to return   65

Conclusion   79

References   89
About the Author   101
About the Inklings series   103

Introduction

I have a vague memory from when I was a child, maybe around six years old, of my brother telling me that our father had been in prison. Of course, at the time I didn't quite understand what it meant, or why he had been imprisoned. I didn't know the concept of 'thought prisoners', a term used in Turkey for those who were convicted of crimes because of their views and the expression of such views. It wasn't until years later that I learned what had happened.

My father had been living in exile in the UK through the '80s, unable to return to Turkey. If he did, he would have faced imprisonment, or worse. It wasn't until October 1989, months before my birth in the UK in February the following year, that he travelled to Turkey to face the charges lobbied against him. The last time he had set foot on his homeland was in 1979, the year before a devastating military coup installed a military junta in

Turkey. My father was accused of many things, including treason, participating in subversive activities against Turkey, degrading Turkey's reputation abroad, and being a communist. Returning at any point would likely mean being arrested and indeed, in months spanning 1989 and 1990, he ended up spending nearly a year in prison, freed only after laws were changed and the articles he was charged under were scrapped from the penal code.

In 2012, my family and I were on a trip to Kos, the Greek Island that's only a 45-minute boat ride from the Turkish coast. You can actually see Turkey's coastline from Kos, it's that close. My father explained that during the years he was exiled within the UK, he would travel to Kos to look across the Mediterranean at the home they couldn't return to. It hit me then, the longing for home that accompanies being in exile.

My father and his friends now freely talk about years they spent living in exile, like it was no big deal. For them it's just part of their history, something that they went through and emerged from on the other side. There is no reason to dwell on the pain. But it is clear that being so far from home has greatly impacted who they have become and their world views. While current younger generations are typically more eager to leave Turkey due to its oppressive politics and crumbling economy, my father's generation is more determined to stay, even as human rights and the quality of life deteriorate every day. When you've been in exile yet able to return safely, it's not surprising that you don't want to leave again, no matter how bad it gets.

After my studies in the US and the UK, I decided to continue living abroad, and my father pointed out how his parents, Gagauz Turks born in Bessarabia, spent most of their lives living abroad in Turkey and how he and my mother also spent years living outside of their home country. He seemed slightly sad that my brother and I would also be spending most of our lives in a foreign country – although our moves were comparatively voluntary.

That's why I want to share the stories of people living in exile. Nowadays, there are a lot of statistics about asylum seekers and refugees and it's depressingly easy to ignore the individuals behind the numbers. Eight people from eight different countries have given me insight into their journeys and I share them with you here. Many of them are living in France as I am currently based in Paris and was able to connect with them through the Agency of Artists in Exile. My aim is to bring the human side back into the story beyond the headlines of waves of immigrants. Although I will share some of those numbers, what truly matters most are the stories of the individuals and what their experiences can tell us about a world obsessed with borders and control.

At the time of writing in 2023, it has been eight years since the infamous image of Alan Kurdi, the two-year-old Syrian boy who drowned in the Mediterranean Sea, made global headlines. You couldn't avoid the photograph of his small, lifeless body laid face-down on a cold shore, plastered all over papers and online. He drowned along with his mother and brother as they tried to leave Turkey amid the European refugee crisis of 2015.[1]

Alan and his family fled the war in Syria to Turkey, hoping to join relatives in Canada. He was among millions trying to enter the European Union using a small inflatable boat. That year, nearly 4,000 refugees died in the eastern Mediterranean.[2]

Although Alan became a symbol and his photograph sparked outrage across the world, immigration has continued to be presented in a negative light by those in power, directly influencing and perpetrating racist public views.[3] One research study found that 54% of Czechs and 51% of Hungarians supported a total ban on the entry of Muslim migrants.[4] In fact, on average, almost one in four Europeans support a ban on Muslim immigration to their country.[5]

In these early 2020s, the UK and the US have stood out amongst countries addressing what they call the 'illegal migration' problem, coming up with 'solutions' that disadvantage legitimate refugees and asylum seekers. In the UK, home secretary Suella Braverman has been outspoken of her disdain towards migrants with the Conservative Party making the negative impacts of 'illegal migration' and 'illegal asylum seekers' a consistent party line.[6] Braverman previously said it is her dream to see a plane full of asylum seekers flown from the UK to Rwanda.[7]

In truth, there is no such thing as an illegal asylum-seeker as every human being has a right to seek asylum in another country under international laws and if a person has applied for asylum, they are not doing so illegally. Regardless, politicians are quick to blame migrants for their countries' various failures. The most visible scapegoats at the moment of writing are arguably those crossing into the UK from Calais via small boats with the government's galling slogan of 'STOP THE BOATS' emblazoned across press junket lecterns.

Meanwhile, under pressure from his far-right opponents, President Emmanuel Macron of France sought to pass new laws to curb immigration. The president has linked immigration to delinquency saying that around half of petty crimes in Paris are being committed by foreigners.[8] The government is looking to pass a bill titled 'Controlling immigration while improving integration', which will expand the scope for deportations and fast-track the asylum application process.[9] The bill has been criticised on both sides of the political spectrum with right-wing politicians disliking the sections that allow the legalisation of undocumented workers and the left-wing politicians claiming it is repressive.[10]

The meaning and psychology of living in exile

Estimates vary but the average length of time people spend in exile can range from 10 years to 26 years.[11] Such prolonged absences and the trauma caused by being forced to leave one's home country, traditionally for political reasons, can have a deep impact on a person's mental health and identity.

There are three main stages of migration that each have a different impact on psychology: pre-migration, transit, and post-migration. Refugees can face various problems at any of these stages, including but not limited to exposure to armed conflict and persecution, detention and lack of access to services, separation from family members, and uncertainty regarding legal status.[12] According to the World Health Organisation, 'factors that negatively impact the mental health and well-being of migrant and refugee children include socioeconomic deprivation, discrimination, racism, low family cohesion, and frequent school changes.'[13] Many refugees will experience distress that can present as anxiety, hopelessness, fatigue, irritability and anger, and although these symptoms largely improve over time, for some, it has a long-lasting impact.

Exile can qualify as a social trauma, and it has been suggested that the process of mourning can help to continue 'being'. Meanwhile, nostalgia can help to protect the ego from inadequacy. However, if nostalgia doesn't evolve beyond looking back, 'the individual enters a depressed state with accompanying feelings of self-pity, resentment, envy, and guilt, which prevents the mourning process from developing.'[14] According to psychologist Dr. Ruth Lijtmaer, when a person arrives as an immigrant or an exile, a psychic depletion can occur and these changes can lead to period of disorganisation, pain, frustration, and a sense of loss.

Such emotions are seen time and time again across refugees, as we'll see in the stories that follow. None arrived in their host country by boat, and they all managed to successfully claim asylum, but that doesn't make their experiences any less difficult. Telling their stories of how they spent their last day in their home country and their experience of settling in a different place is an attempt to move beyond the tabloid headlines. Their stories are difficult but exemplary of finding hope in despair and, as Litjmaer says, discovering 'new possibilities and a hopeful future'.

Chapter 1

Can you feel at home in a foreign country?

A failed abduction and a dissident

Taha Siddiqui was in a taxi heading to the airport in Pakistan's capital Islamabad just as he had done countless times before travelling to London for work. They were taking the main expressway when a car screeched to a stop in front of the taxi and four men tumbled out, armed with AK-47s. They were there to abduct Taha.

Taha, a prominent, award-winning journalist in Pakistan, worked for a number of different publications including the *New York Times*, the *Guardian* and *France 24*. He was known as a critic of the country's military, so security agencies kept a close watch on his work, often calling him and harassing him over articles he published.

The men dragged him out of the taxi and beat him, threatening to shoot him multiple times if he didn't cooperate. Forced into the vehicle as it pulled away, Taha noticed that the door on the other side was unlocked. Seeing his chance, he jumped out while the car was moving. Although he tried to get help from a military vehicle passing by, it was useless – one of the abductors just gestured for the military vehicle to continue driving and they obliged. Taha knew he had to get away and continued to run into oncoming traffic, finally jumping into a taxi that drove him at least a few hundred metres away from his assailants. When he got out, he ran through ditches along the highway until he was out of sight and free to hide.

A few months before the abduction attempt, Taha had complained of being harassed by Pakistan's security services. While many would have shut up after such an attack, it didn't deter Taha. 'The attack happened and that was January 10th, 2018. Right after the attack I started giving interviews, speaking a lot and I got some messages from journalist friends who played on both sides of the fence. They told me, "the military is really angry, even after all this you're not shutting up",' he recalls to me during our interview. He thought that next time, instead of an abduction, they will probably shoot him on the spot. For Taha, there is no question that this was the Pakistani military's doing.

Ten days after the attempted abduction, the Interior Minister called him to say that the government doesn't have anything against him. However, he also warned that in the run up to elections, meant to take place in July 2018, an interim government would take power and they would not be able to protect him. Taha had police protection after the attack but that would be pulled back once the interim government took over. When he questioned the Interior Minister, Taha was told, 'the military has a big problem with you and you should, in my opinion, go quiet and apologise to the military. Write a letter of apology to the army chief.' Taha wasn't even sure what he would apologise for even if he wanted to. But the Minister insisted that Taha should issue a blanket apology, just to save himself. In Pakistan, the Interior Minister is at the top of the military food chain. Technically, the Chief of the Armed Services reports to him, but the Minister was telling Taha to apologise to his subordinate.

Taha gave me some insight into how he coped under this pressure. 'Some of my friends were already telling me it's better if I take a break because I was under trauma. I had flashback issues, post-traumatic stress disorder (PTSD). I started seeing a therapist, but she told me I should see the good side of the military. I was shocked. I wasn't there to listen to justifications of the military's oppressive power. I was having psychological issues with what happened, I was wronged but everyone was telling me that I was wrong.'

Pakistan is one of the deadliest countries in the world for journalists, with three to four murders each year, according to Reporters Without Borders. It ranks 157 out of 180 on the World Press Freedom Index.[15] While this was not the first time Taha faced a powerful foe, it was the most extreme. The previous year, the counter-terrorism wing of the government called Taha in for interrogation due to his work, but Taha bravely took the Federal Investigation Agency to court for harassing him and trying to intimidate him.

The government directly controls the country's media regulators and with the military's tight grip over government institutions, any coverage against it is off limits. There are several laws that are used to censor criticism of the government and the armed forces, including the Prevention of Electronic Crimes Act passed in 2016 that was used against Taha. As these Acts are vaguely worded, journalists can often find themselves in breach and are easy to target, with the threat of heavy administrative and criminal penalties, including prison sentences.

With this high-profile case, and now the abduction attempt, Taha's bosses were worried, telling him to back down. Seeing that he wasn't going to, they requested he take a break, at least until the elections. Taha had several options to escape the threats against his livelihood and his life. He had worked for American, British, and French publications and although the first two were preferable because of the language, the French embassy was the first one to respond and start work on getting him a visa.

'When I was attacked, they took my passport so I had to get a new one. The government helped me. But publicly they were saying they had nothing to do with me. Pakistan is very dysfunctional like that. One end of the government will help you and the other will screw you. I was getting police protection while the military was trying to kill me,' he explained.

The French embassy said the visa would take around five to seven days, but it was successfully processed quickly, allowing Taha to plan accordingly.

'I was really paranoid thinking they will come and kill me. At the time, anyone who wanted to talk about the media under suppression was talking to me. I was one of the most vocal people after the attack,' he said. 'Most go quiet. Although not everyone has a choice to leave. I was privileged to have that choice.'

Taha didn't tell anyone that he was going to leave. He asked his partner if she would go with him, and she agreed. Their son was just over four years old at the time. In that week, while waiting for the visas, they had to get rid of their belongings and figure out what to do with their house. They gave most of their furniture to another journalist who had just moved to the country.

'Basically, I had to throw things away, leave stuff, memories and things. A week ago, we never would have thought that we would want to leave, and we were now leaving. We disposed of what we had, we had cars we had to sell off. My son was in school, and it was the middle of the school year. I talked to him about it and he started crying.' He was understandably sad about leaving behind his friends and eventually he asked if he could at least take his toys with him – which is how they ended up with a suitcase full of toys when they finally left Pakistan.

With the recent abduction attempt still haunting Taha, travelling to the airport was triggering. They were under police protection, but Taha felt he couldn't trust them fully.

'The police were travelling with us as well going to the airport. I was under severe trauma from the last time. There was a police car in the front and back. Until we reached the airport, I told the policemen I'm going to Karachi. When I made them stop at the international side they said, "this is international departures". I just smiled but didn't say anything to them. I went to Qatar airlines, got a flight to Paris and arrived the night of 13th of February, 2018.'

Getting out of Pakistan was one thing, but resettling in Paris and living abroad was something else. The threats against him didn't stop and he was still very much afraid. At least 42 journalists have been killed in Pakistan in the last four years[16] but the displaced haven't always been protected from their original threats, either. In 2020

Sajid Hussein, Pakistani journalist and the founder and chief editor of the online news site, the *Balochistan Times*, who had been living in exile in Sweden was found dead in a river. In October 2022, Pakistani journalist, writer, and television news anchor Arshad Sharif, another critic of the army, was shot dead in Kenya.

Several months after Taha had arrived in France he was invited to a conference in the US as a speaker. At this time, Pakistan's elections had taken place and Imran Khan was elected Prime Minister. With the interim government gone, Taha was mulling over whether it was safe to go back. His answer came when he arrived in the US and received a call from the FBI, asking to meet. They told Taha that his name was on a kill list that they intercepted, mentioned in communications from Pakistan following the elections. If he went back to Pakistan, in his mind, it was certain that he would be killed. If he went to any country that had friendly relations with Pakistan, he could be extradited. This was around the same time that Jamal Khashoggi, Saudi dissident journalist, was assassinated by agents of the Saudi government at the country's consulate in Istanbul. FBI agents warned Taha that this could embolden other states to take similar actions.

When he returned to France, French intelligence agencies confirmed the FBI's information. Taha was informed his parents also got a visit back home in Pakistan telling them that Taha should stop talking or they would be in trouble. Since then, they've had multiple visits and threats.

Aside from government pressure, Taha was also dealing with a disinformation campaign. People in Pakistan falsely claimed that he fabricated his attempted abduction and consequent threats because he simply wanted to live abroad and be granted asylum. On the other hand, his friends insisted he had a career in Pakistan, was known as a successful journalist and would become irrelevant if he didn't return.

All Taha could think about was how to stay alive to tell his story.

'At that point in time I didn't want to think about the future. If I think about the future, it's uncertain. The future is unpredictable. I am a person that stresses about the future, but at that time I trained my mind to not ask questions. If I do that, I'll go crazy, wondering what will happen,' he recalled.

Now, he doesn't think that he can ever go back.

'Given the fact that I've become much more vocal, Pakistan has become a lot more oppressive. I've been contacted by the military and been told that I should come back, they will forget about it. But I know what their true intentions are. So, I think maybe when I'm older and calmer maybe I stop speaking, or maybe when Pakistan changes,' he said.

'Also, now that I'm out of Pakistan, I realise we were

living in a very dysfunctional country. Nation states are a bad idea and Pakistan is a really bad idea. It's an Islamic republic, which makes no sense. You live there and it's a great story to tell. But I have a child, I'm anti-theist, I speak openly against Islam, religion.

'I couldn't fit into Pakistan, it was very difficult for me to fit in with the freedom of expression issue and religion issue. It was overwhelmingly oppressive. Now I look back, people ask if I miss it. Why should I miss something which is dysfunctional, which is a wrong idea to begin with? I miss my family and friends, I miss people. But they can visit me and we can meet somewhere else.'

Taha now owns The Dissident Club in Paris, a small bar where dissidents of the world can meet. He runs events, brings outsiders together and works to help other people in exile in France. Adjusting to life in this new environment wasn't easy but Taha's son helped him find the strength he needed, and he now realises how resilient children are. His son is now nine years old and has spent half of his life in France.

'In retrospect he was the one that really helped us feel like it's okay to have this change. He gave us – in my case at least – strength in making me feel like if the kid can do it why can't I do it?'

Being a political refugee in France and running the club has also brought up a lot of questions around identity for Taha. He found that many political refugees actively didn't want to identify as such because the term 'refugee' carries such negative connotations due to the ongoing media narrative representing them as a problem. When he told people he was a political refugee he would get asked if he came over on a boat.

'Here, in France, if you're a political refugee, people would be pitying you. That's why people don't identify themselves as a political refugee at times. You don't feel like you have any rights as a citizen. You feel scared to do anything and are on the back foot all the time.'

There is also a feeling that you owe something to the country hosting you. It took Taha some time to understand that seeking asylum is a fundamental right protected by the UN in the Geneva Convention and it's not being granted as a favour.

'I've taken pride in my situation. When people tell me, "you're from Pakistan", I tell them I'm a political refugee and I make them understand what this means. My idea is also to sensitize people, they're desensitized to what a political refugee is. It's not just because you're living in a war situation that you leave. People leave for different reasons.

'Here in France now I feel like I want to own up to my identity as a political refugee, as someone in exile because I think that's who I am, and I should own it. I shouldn't be ashamed of it in any way. Even though those were the thoughts I had initially.'

While Taha has something of a happy ending, in the last few years there have been numerous alerts for other Pakistanis in exile by security services in the UK, the US, France and the Netherlands. In early 2022, a London-based hitman was found guilty of conspiracy to murder Pakistani dissident Ahmed Waqas Goraya, who criticised the Inter-Services Intelligence, the country's intelligence agency.[17] In France, journalist Yunas Khan received an email from French authorities telling him about leaked files where a figure from Pakistan's ruling party tells the community in Europe to attack him.[18]

But the attacks on dissidents have moved beyond threats, with several being killed, despite being granted political asylum in the West. Karima Baloch, who fled Pakistan in 2015 due to her work as a human rights activist was found dead in Canada in 2021.[19] Taha's terrifying journey is just one of thousands, with most not as ultimately lucky as him. According to UNHCR data, nearly 25,000 people fled from Pakistan in 2021 and applied for asylum in other countries. By mid-2022, there were 123,218 refugees from Pakistan, with 58,244 of those seeking asylum.[20]

A nationality stripped

Palestinian-Egyptian activist Ramy Shaath was arrested by Egyptian security forces on July 5th, 2019. That was the last time he saw his home. As a child he was political beyond his years, likely due to his father being active in Palestinian politics. Ramy gave rousing weekly speeches at his school in Egypt as young as 10 years old. He had his first run-in with the security forces at 11 when he was called in to the headmistress's office where a colonel in the state security services informed him that he was no longer allowed to make his speeches. Undeterred, Ramy grew up attending protests, organising medication collections for fighters in Lebanon, giving yet more speeches to those who needed it. By the end of the '80s and early '90s he was in university when the first Iraq war as well as the first Palestinian Intifada, a series of uprisings in the Palestinian territories and Israel, had started.

Reaction to his actions from the Egyptian regime encouraged him to fight for democracy and human rights in Egypt. 'I am equally Egyptian and Palestinian. There is nothing that is good for Egypt that would be bad for Palestine, so for me those two identities are the one and the same,' he told me. 'And it became this duality, fighting for Palestine and democracy in Egypt. For me it's the same fight.'

His first official arrest in 1990 came for his protesting.

'I remember the first question they asked me. "Are you a communist or are you from the Islamic movement?"' he recalled. Even at the time he found this hilarious and suggested the arresting officers to put his file under both groups if they didn't know who he's siding with.

Ramy later became close to Yasser Arafat, chairman of the Palestine Liberation Organization from 1969 to 2004 and President of the Palestinian National Authority from 1994 to 2004. He worked with Arafat from 1992 until 1998 during which time he lived in Gaza, but by the end he was disenchanted with the Palestinian Authority due to a lack of vision, widespread corruption and extreme weakness in confronting the Israelis, he reveals. After having a fight with Arafat, he left Palestine and moved back to Egypt.

'I returned to Egypt and my old mode of advocating for Palestine while fighting for Egyptian democracy. The 2000s was a hot period for Egypt and a disaster for Palestine. Eventually, after Arafat died in 2004, the new guy came, who I hated. He was extremely bad and weak, and ruined whatever was left of the organisation.'

Ramy explained that at the end of the 2000s they started preparing for a revolution in Egypt. Between 2011 and 2013 he was out on the streets at demonstrations, organising people and sit-ins. Although it seemed like the revolutionary movement was winning initially, Ramy said he knew they were not yet at the point of destroying the regime. Through all his work he was envisioning creating a civil, independent, and democratic country. The cause for the revolution was decided as 'bread, freedom and social justice'.[21]

'Since the mid-70s Egypt has been under complete American control and hegemony. It is very warm towards the Israelis as well. That's ruining Egypt's ability to realise its resources, its economy and national security in the right way. So political independence from American and Israeli control was a main cause as well,' Ramy explained.

By mid-2013 there was a coup d'état in Egypt that brought general Abdel Fattah al-Sisi to power. Ramy tried to regroup the revolutionary movement into the revolutionary front but the military government was coming down hard on any dissent. 'It was the first time we were faced with machine guns and tanks in a demonstration. In one day, I had 350 of my guys arrested. It became very difficult to be in the streets, but we kept fighting and organising in different ways.'

That's when Ramy co-founded the Boycott, Divestment and Sanctions (BDS) movement in Egypt, to end international support for Israel's oppression of Palestinians. In his view it cut across causes in both countries as not only was it boycotting companies benefiting from the Israeli occupation of Palestine, it also helped reveal corruption in Egypt. Every time there was a deal between an Israeli company and Egypt, the counter party was a general in the security forces, revealing the corruption inside the security apparatus and the army.

It also acted as a unifying group among Egypt's opposition. Following Sisi's rise to power in 2013, the opposition in Egypt was desperate. The military regime targeted both the Islamic movement and the revolutionary movement. For BDS, Ramy gathered the ten opposition political parties, all the revolutionary movements, and different non-governmental organisations. It became the only meeting that gathered all the forces of the opposition around one table.

'That was bothering the regime extremely as it was able to destroy everything else,' Rami explained proudly. The BDS movement forced many companies to leave Israel including France's Orange. Ramy also continued to work on putting together a political front to face the regime.

'Every day I expected I would be arrested. I knew it was coming but I wasn't sure when. At that point they clearly thought I was too expensive to arrest because I'm a known name. I got some calls from state security and the intelligence service saying my name will appear in a case the next day so I should leave the country immediately. I told them they know my home address they can come pick me up when they want.'

By 2018, Ramy wondered if they were never going to arrest him, so he continued to up the ante. That's when the so-called 'deal of the century' was announced by US president Donald Trump. It was a plan, put together by Trump's son-in-law Jared Kushner, to solve the Israeli-Palestinian conflict. It was described by many as a smokescreen to allow the annexation of most of the West Bank by Israel.[22] Ramy knew he had to fight it even though it might be the end of his good luck.

On the June 25th, 2019, the first official meeting for the 'deal of the century' was held in Bahrain. Ramy organised a conference for the same time in Beirut with the opposition from all the Arab countries including the Emirates, Egypt, Morocco, Algeria, and Lebanon. At that meeting he revealed the Egyptian participation in the deal with documents he had obtained. Two days after he returned to Egypt, his luck ran out and Ramy was arrested.

That morning, Ramy had work, some meetings and then went home to prepare to travel again in three days' time to attend his daughter's graduation in Leeds, UK. He was working at home on a speech he was planning on giving soon and his wife, Celine, was out. Just after midnight, she came back home, parked the car, and noticed that the neighbourhood was surrounded by soldiers and tanks. Roads were in the process of being blocked. She called Ramy and said, 'they're coming for you, they're here'.

Before they could break it down, Ramy opened the door for the men who would eventually arrest him. Two officers and around ten soldiers entered his house. Instead of searching the house, as he expected, they stood around aimlessly. After some time Ramy asked the officers what they were waiting for, jokingly offering them coffee. It turned out they were waiting for the general, who arrived minutes later. Ramy started laughing, though this made the general angry, he says, who informed him of the seriousness of the situation.

'I asked him why I was being arrested and he said he didn't know, the order came from high up. That was the first indication I had that it was the president's decision, not the security service.'

They gave his wife, a French citizen, five minutes to pack her things as she would be deported. Under gunpoint, Ramy and Celine said their goodbyes. They were put in two different cars with one headed to the airport and the other to what Ramy called 'forced disappearance'. That was the last time he was in downtown Cairo, in the home he had lived in for 40 years. He spent the next two and a half years in prison.

It was only after significant international pressure and stripping Ramy of his Egyptian citizenship that he was released. 'I was only able to get my Palestinian documentation after 1994 and now they took my Egyptian nationality. So, for the first 23 years of my life, the occupation refused my nationality and now a dictatorship took the other one,' Ramy joked. 'But neither of them decides who I am. I don't care about the documents. And the day this Sisi dictator falls, I will be in Cairo regaining my nationality,' he declared. 'It is not their document that decides who I am or what I do. It is a vulgar, illegal action.'

Exile is, unfortunately, a familiar concept to Palestinians. In 1948, more than 700,000 Palestinian Arabs, making up over half the population, were expelled or voluntarily fled from their homeland following the establishment of the State of Israel. With the support of the British government, Israel was declared an independent state, triggering the first Arab-Israeli war. Referred to as 'Nakba' (catastrophe), Israeli military forces captured nearly 80% of historic Palestine. The rest was divided into what is now the occupied West Bank and the Gaza Strip.

Numerous reasons are cited through history for the Palestinian exodus and it is still subject to some controversy. Some say that the destruction of Arab villages and the fear of massacres following the Deir Yassin village attack that massacred more than 110 people, led to Arabs fleeing their homes. But Israel has claimed that they left because they were ordered to by their own leaders.

In the aftermath of the Six-Day War less than twenty years later in 1967, around 250,000 people fled, with Israel capturing additional territory, occupying the Gaza Strip and the West Bank, including East Jerusalem. A 1971 UN Special Committee report concluded that the Government of Israel was 'deliberately carrying out policies aimed at preventing the population of the occupied territories from returning to their homes and forcing those who are in their homes in the occupied territories to leave, either by direct means such as deportation or indirectly by attempts at undermining their morale or through the offer of special inducements'.

In a 2021 article, American-Palestinian journalist Ramzy Baroud provided an apt description of what exile is for Palestinians. 'For Palestinians, exile is not simply the physical act of being removed from their homes and denied the chance to return. It is not a casual topic pertaining to politics and international law either. Nor is it an ethereal notion, a sentiment, or a poetic verse. It is all these combined.'

By the end of 2022, the number of Palestinians around the world had reached 14.3 million, according to the Palestinian Central Bureau of Statistics. Five million of those are living within the 1967 borders and 2.2 million are in the Gaza strip. With seven million people living abroad, Palestinians make up one of the largest diaspora populations in the world. This number has increased significantly, mainly because the descendants of refugees from Palestine are also considered refugees by the UN Relief and Works Agency.

Meanwhile, since 2013, Egypt sent its fair share of people into exile. There are up to 14 million Egyptians living abroad and of these tens of thousands are living in exile. In addition, an estimated 60,000 people are political prisoners in the country.

Ramy is not the first to be stripped of his citizenship. The government's crackdown on any dissent has been brutal. Activist Ghada Naguib's citizenship was revoked in 2020, becoming the first to be stripped of her nationality over her criticisms of Sisi's government. A Human Rights Watch report found that Egyptian authorities have been refusing to provide or renew identity documents of dozens of dissidents, activists and journalists living abroad, to pressure them to return to the country.[23]

Ramy has already filed a suit against Egypt in the regional African court but is ready to go to international courts if needed. In exile, he's using his freedom to speak about Egypt and Palestine. He is working on making it harder for European governments to turn a blind eye, he said. 'I'm hitting them very hard. It has been very effective in changing the understanding of the dictatorship in Egypt and the language. I always believed that those regimes are there because of Western complicity and support. So, I concentrated more and more on making it more difficult for them to publicly meet him and support him. It's also making it hard for him to get loans from outside,' he explained.

Although he is continuing the fight, he does have a bit of survivor's guilt. Therefore, he is also helping people escape Egypt. Ramy has been in France since he got out of prison. When he was first arrested, he was told that it was a combined Egyptian, Emirati and Israeli decision with a green light from the Americans and so he would never get out. Eventually, after two and a half years and long negotiations they took him to an underground cell before a plane to Jordan and then to France. Although he's been in Nanterre since January 2022, he says he was thinking more long-term when he was in prison as he struggles to accept that his stay in France might last many years.

While a part of him is easily integrating and he has been welcomed by the local people and governments, part of him is still resisting. He is refusing to learn French and although he can apply for citizenship, he so far has chosen not to. He has also refused to apply for asylum, acting as though France is just a transit country and not his final destination.

'Part of me is still resisting the idea of me being here. Part of my daily work and soul is between Cairo and Palestine, whether talking to people and indulging in politics. Of course, I realise where I am and how that allows me to do things in terms of freedom of speech, that others in Egypt cannot do,' he said. But he realises that until there is a change in leadership in Egypt, he will not be able to return. Until that happens he will continue the fight.

Chapter 2
Those who didn't know

Second time in exile

When Afghanistan's borders finally opened in mid-2021 after the travel restrictions of the COVID-19 pandemic, Dr. Sima Samar desperately wanted to travel to the US to see her children, who had relocated there permanently years before. It had been more than a year and a half since she last saw them. She packed as she normally would for a trip and arrived in the US on the 25th of June, 2021. Her return ticket was booked for the 10th of August. She didn't know when she was getting on that plane that this would be her last day in her home country of Afghanistan.

Sima is a prominent, multi award-winning women's and human rights advocate, who was previously a doctor at the government hospital in Kabul when her husband was arrested in 1979. With her young son, she fled to

Pakistan and never saw her husband again. She lived in exile in Pakistan for seventeen years and established a hospital for Afghan refugee women, until a US-led invasion drove the Taliban from power, allowing her to return home. Doing so in 2001, hoping to rebuild Afghanistan's infrastructure, she became the Deputy Prime Minister in Hamid Karzai's government and from December 2001 to 2003 she served as the Minister of Women's Affairs. Throughout her impressive career, Sima has dedicated her livelihood to restoring women's rights in Afghanistan, improving their lives in the process. Despite receiving death threats for questioning conservative Islamic laws, so much so that she was forced to resign from her post, she worked tirelessly as a champion of women's rights.

In 2019, she was appointed as a member of the United Nations Secretary-General's High-Level Panel on Internal Displacement and served as special envoy of the President of Afghanistan and State Minister for Human Rights and International Affairs before that. But on that day in June 2021, all those positions and accolades paled in comparison to her role as mother, looking forward to seeing her children and family after a long, difficult absence.

Earlier in April, the US administration had announced its decision to pull out all troops from Afghanistan by September and after Sima's arrival in the US, the situation on the ground in Afghanistan deteriorated fast. She postponed her return for two weeks until late August and in that time, Afghan president Ashraf Ghani fled the country, the Taliban taking power for the second time.

'I didn't have an official job at the time, I was doing some other work that was non-governmental, which is why I was coming to stay for six weeks in the US,' she said. 'When I left, it was a normal day so I came here very normally. Although the security situation was very bad, so I was careful.'

Although Afghanistan had many problems while Sima lived there and life was rarely comfortable, she wishes she could go home because, in the end, it is her own country. While she misses it, she has understandable anger as to how Afghanistan could have ended up in its troubled state. 'How can you leave the country and 35 million people in the hands of this group of people? The international community should not just watch. Because in my view it was a collective failure, so it should be dealt with collectively, rather than just playing the blame game, which is not very helpful,' she said.

'I'm not saying we shouldn't be blamed. We should be, because each one of us should be blamed and should be held accountable for our actions. But we need to find a solution because the problem in Afghanistan will not stay inside the borders of Afghanistan. Before it becomes a very tough and harsh issue, we should take some action.'

When she had to postpone her return flight, she cried. 'I had a really difficult time because I was not thinking that I would stay in the US forever and that I would be applying for asylum in another country at this age,' she said.

Many Afghans are used to living in exile (or the threat of living in exile), first after the 1979 Soviet invasion and then following the Taliban's 1996 takeover, leading to decades of war and instability for its civilians. It's not just Sima who fled Afghanistan. Much of the population lived in exile, primarily in Pakistan, until the US invasion in 2001.

In 2016, there was a huge uptick in the number of Afghan refugees returning from Pakistan, with more than 370,000 going back, according to UNHCR data.[24] But many have had to leave again after the US completed its withdrawal from the country on 30th August, 2021 and the Taliban took control of the country.

Possibly unsurprisingly, Afghanistan is one of the leading countries in the world to create refugees. By the end of 2021, 3.5 million Afghans were forcibly displaced from their homes within the country, and 2.6 million were hosted as refugees.[25] Most recently in January 2023, according to the European Union Agency for Asylum, Afghans lodged 12,100 applications to EU+ countries, up 42% year-on-year, and representing 13% of all applications in Europe. Of these, only 2,900 were granted refugee status. Afghans were the largest group to make asylum applications, second only to Syrians.[26]

In the first few months of 2023, two-thirds of Afghanistan's population, around 28.3 million people, needed humanitarian and protection assistance. More than 8.2 million Afghans have been driven out of their homes and into neighbouring countries, with 85% refugees living in Pakistan and Iran. More than 70% of all displaced Afghans within the country are women and children.[27]

As Sima was not arriving in the US as part of the evacuation of Afghanistan, she went through a different immigration process. A friend helped her get a visa so she could work, and she was sponsored by Harvard University as a visiting scholar. Eventually she was able to apply for a green card.

For others, obtaining the right to stay in the US has been more difficult. Majority of applications, some 90%, from Afghans to enter the US on humanitarian grounds have been rejected.[28]

Meanwhile, a group of Afghan people seeking asylum are suing the US government because of delays in processing their applications.[29]

In addition to the struggles of the Afghan people in the US, asylum seekers from other nationalities have also been met with increased hostility. President Joe Biden's administration published a proposed rule in

February 2023 that would essentially ban many from seeking asylum in the United States, with focus on the US-Mexico border. Similar to the approach the UK is trying to take, the rule would make refugees ineligible for asylum based on their manner of entry, so if an asylum seeker crossed another country on their way to the US, they would be banned from applying in the US unless they previously applied for and were denied asylum in that other country. The International Rescue Committee noted that 'these requirements are unfeasible and impractical for many people in need of protection, as some asylum seekers cannot find safety in the countries where they first arrive because of violence or persecution similar to that in their native land'.[30]

In a note, the Committee added, 'Most asylum seekers travel to the US through Mexico, which is already one of the largest recipients of asylum applications. Although a viable country for some asylum seekers, the country faces record levels of violence and is not a safe place for many.'

The new rules came into effect in May. Two months after the asylum ban, not-for-profit organisation Human Rights First interviewed more than 300 people seeking asylum in Mexico. It found that the ban endangers lives by leaving them waiting in Mexico where they can be targeted for kidnapping, rape, and exploitation. It found that Black, Indigenous and LGBTQ+ people were particularly disadvantaged when seeking asylum.

The policy has been called Trump-esque[31] as it closely resembles asylum policies adopted when Donald Trump was president.

In addition to national policies there have also been anti-immigrant action in states. Florida lawmakers approved a legislation that will hand Governor Ron DeSantis millions to transport migrants out of the state.[32] DeSantis announced his candidacy for president in May 2023 and revealed that a crackdown on illegal immigration would be at the top of his agenda.[33] His proposals include sending the US military to the border and the mass detention of undocumented people. In addition, he revived Trump's promise to build a wall at the southern border.[34]

Texas governor Greg Abbott, following in DeSantis' footsteps, shipped 40 immigrants to California.[35] He said that border towns in Texas are still 'overrun' with migrants and his drop-offs of over 17,500 migrants in cities including Chicago, New York City, Philadelphia, and Washington, DC, was a response to President Biden failing to secure the borders.[36]

Like the UK, the US has special resettlement schemes for people from Afghanistan and Ukraine. The Uniting for Ukraine program, announced in April 2022, is a new streamlined process for Ukranians fleeing the Russian invasion.[37] And Afghans were previously able to enter the US under the humanitarian parole authority – which allows them to live temporarily in the US without fear of deportation.[38] This ended in October 2022, with the Biden administration instead announcing that it would focus on providing a pathway to permanent legal status.[39] These programs have had their own set of issues.

For Sima, her second time in exile is not easy, but it's human nature to adapt as much as possible, even if the new situation is unthinkable. And at least she can stay in the US for now and continue working.

'Each one of us have our own way of feeling and our own problems, and at the end of the day, even if you are living in a poor country in a difficult situation, it's your country and you have freedom there,' she said. 'I never thought I would be pushed to apply for asylum.'

But she firmly believes change will come and as Pablo Neruda, one of the 20th century's most influential poets once wrote, *you can cut all the flowers but you cannot keep spring from coming.* 'They [the Taliban] have been killing people, and people will disappear as much as they want but they cannot really stop resistance,' she said. 'They cannot turn Afghanistan into a graveyard without any protest or resistance against it.'

Sima is not unique in living in exile for a second time. Many Afghans were sadly forced to leave their country a second time since Taliban's takeover in 2021. Repatriation after a period of exile typically puts an end to uncertainty and provides an opportunity to rebuild. It gives hope. For that hope to be crushed once again, after years of hard work rebuilding both your own life and your country, as Sima has done, can be shocking.

When it's illegal to be who you are

Ahmed's[40] face and body, blurry and torn, appear in photographs and paintings digitally layered, reflected on an image of a relative. That is just one of his works of art. He says he's not a specialist in one medium or another, but his art reflects his experience living between two cultures.

Forced to leave Morocco due to his sexual orientation and freedom of expression issues, Ahmed is an artist, creating installations, as well as a poet.

'There is certainly a literary dimension to my work, introspective writing made manifest through visual arts. The rest of the time, I just have three and a half jobs and do my best to assert myself and navigate a system that is still largely discriminating without ever dwelling on victimhood or accepting my identity to be fractured and reduced to a traumatic moment... It's a lot of micro acts of resistance in the everyday life that are not to be excluded of my artistic experience,' he explained.

Born in Morocco, Ahmed grew up on the family farm, just a few kilometres away from his grandfather's house. When he left for France at the end of the summer of 2014 he didn't know that he wouldn't be going back.

After studying at a School of Fine Arts, Ahmed moved to France to continue his studies. He went on holiday with his family that summer, they were all there, something that never happened. It was as if the whole family had gathered to see Ahmed one last time. He doesn't remember the day of his departure from Morocco. For him it wasn't anything unusual, he was just going back to school. But he remembers that holiday, when all his loved ones were together.

Back in France, he decided to find a job there, not as an asylum-seeker but as a post-grad, using the six months the government gives international students after graduating to settle and find themselves a job. Interview after interview, Ahmed wasn't successful. He was told on numerous occasions that it was easier for the employer to hire a French candidate rather than sponsor him, a costly process both financially and in admin. With time running out on his six-month window, he couldn't find a job but didn't want to go back to Morocco either, for fear of persecution and attack, so applied for asylum and, thankfully, was successful.[41]

'I was lucky that it didn't take a long time for me to get it, but I was really honest. I told them I want to work here and for obvious reasons I can't be how I want to be [back home],' he said. Ahmed was lucky getting his asylum application approved, as many Moroccans have struggled. Compared with Syria or Afghanistan, there aren't that many people applying for asylum from Morocco.

In 2022, the Spanish Office on Asylum and Refuge rejected 3,542 applications out of the 3,905 requests submitted, likely because in some countries, Morocco is considered a safe country of origin for asylum seekers, which means that their cases are processed more quickly, and typically unsuccessfully.[42]

In 2021, there were 14,929 who left Morocco and applied for asylum in other countries, according to UNHCR data. That's just around 0.040% of all residents. And 91% of applications were rejected.[43] Moroccan Association of Human Rights estimates that there are currently around 20,000 Moroccans living in exile.

The assumption that Morocco is a safe country to reside has been widely disputed and there are those who still face human rights abuses within the country. Human rights abuse in Morocco has recently come under the spotlight when the European Parliament adopted its first resolution in twenty-five years criticising Morocco on the situation of journalists in the country.[44] According to a Human Rights Watch report published in 2022, dozens of journalists and activists critical of Morocco's author-ities have been convicted on charges of publishing false news or defaming local officials. In addition, author-ities have increasingly accused high-profile journalists of sexual crimes.[45]

Ahmed has lived in France for nearly 10 years. It's difficult for him to think of what he's left behind, saying he mostly misses his childhood. 'Being young and careless, discovering everything for the first time. Being excited about the world. Those feelings stay with you, build the beginning of your patterns and personality, so you come back to them,' he said.

Growing up he was always more independent.

'Maybe also because I'm gay, there is a big part of loneliness that I couldn't really connect with people and find people who were like me. I learned to navigate life independently when I was very young. But I didn't know it was because of my sexuality, as a teenager I just didn't know. It's hard to figure out the world.'

Ahmed knows a lot of people who call their parents every day, who rely on them while growing up, so when they lose it, they feel that gap a lot more. Although he loves his parents and knows that they love him, he learned to take care of his emotional needs by himself. He came out when he was around twenty years old, and his parents said they were okay.

'I only care about the things I can control,' he explained. 'I did what I had to do and it's up to them. I don't think about things that involve other people, even if it's my family. I just focus on the fact that we love each other and that's enough. Culturally we don't speak a lot about those things and sometimes I think it's even better.

Not everyone has to aspire to be gay like the French. That's problematic in the West – they want everyone to come out. We don't speak about things, but we accept things. It's smoother in a way. We don't have to shout about it. That would feel uncomfortable from a Western perspective, but we don't speak about them and I don't feel bad about that.'

He points out that homophobic laws were brought to Morocco by the French colonial system. 'We didn't have this constitution before the French came and brought homophobic laws. I wouldn't go to jail like I would now, and I wouldn't have to be a refugee,' he said. The conflict Ahmed feels between two cultures goes back far beyond his own time, into other cultures in his history.

Being gay is illegal in Morocco, punishable by up to three years in prison as well as a fine. One report published in 2013 estimated that nearly 5,000 men had been arrested and thrown in jail since 1956.[46] Morocco is just one country where same-sex sexual activity is penalised, there are 67 jurisdictions where private and consensual same-sex sexual activity is criminalised.[47] In 11 of those countries, the death penalty can be imposed, including in Iran, Saudi Arabia and Somalia. In 14 countries, the expression of transgender identity is criminalised.[48]

Seeking asylum based on sexual orientation remains difficult. According to research from the University of Sussex, one in three LGBT+ asylum seekers see their claims rejected because officials don't believe them.[49] Even when their asylum claims are granted, they can still face discrimination in their host country. In the US, LGBT+ people are four times more likely to experience violence.[50]

Ahmed's relationship with his grandfather informed his early years. He was a Berber (an indigenous group and the oldest inhabitants of North Africa) who grew up in Casablanca and the first generation in his family to speak Arabic after the Arab invasion in the seventh century changed the demographics in Morocco and converted Berbers to Islam. At various times there have been tensions between the two groups.

Although his grandfather was Berber, Ahmed never learned the language. When he visited other Berbers they would think he was ashamed, but it was just that he grew up in a more Arabised culture. 'It is an identity that was complex to start with and now there is another layer – a Moroccan living in France. All the differences that exist, how you never feel like you belong anywhere. I don't really know any Moroccans here… [Once] I was so happy I met all these Moroccan artists, but it's complicated to connect, because everyone is trying to prove themselves in this society, so they don't have time for community,' he explained.

There is also a difference between French people with a Moroccan background and Moroccans living in

France. The former are already French, therefore they feel entitled and go back to their communities. 'I would be lying if I said I belong 100% to those communities. They idealise Morocco too much, they hate France. I'm not going to say there aren't problems but maybe I don't have the same point of view. It's a different experience. It's not easy, it's complex and rich that we have to understand all these things, deal with them.'

Risk of imprisonment

Rezvan Zahedi remembers sitting in the courtyard at her parents' house in Iran, surrounded by lemon trees, drinking tea with her father. Every time, her father gets up to take a lemon for their tea and they continue their conversations for hours. She hasn't been back in nearly eight years and misses it dearly.

Rezvan was born in 1987, in Booshehr, Iran. At the age of twenty, she began her career as a photographer and graffiti artist. She worked with a group of artists, graffitiing buildings at night, depicting scenes and statements against Iran's regime. While one group was working on the art, another would function as lookout. If they got caught, the punishment would be severe. Although their confrontive pieces would usually be removed by the government within 24 hours, she was proud of the work they did.

During the day, Rezvan worked on ceramics, a more acceptable art form in the Islamic Republic. Under the cover of night, Rezvan could practice her *real* art. The ceramics provided a useful cover as during evening excursions, she would always carry her work badge and flyers for the company, pretending to put up advertising if anyone asked what she was doing.

She couldn't really exhibit her photographs while in Iran, although had some clandestine shows open only to really close friends and family. Her ideas come from her life in Iran, particularly the oppression of women. In Iran, women are severely restricted from social life. From the age of nine they are forced to cover their hair and face restrictions on their dress. The legal age of marriage is 13 and women do not have the right to divorce. There are also severe restrictions on foreign travel, inheritance, and child custody. Breaking the rules carry extremely harsh sentences. For example, women not wearing the hijab could be sentenced to 10 days to two months in prison. Speaking out against the government, considered as insulting the leadership, can lead to a prison sentence of six months to two years. Protestors have recently been sentenced to death, convicted of the offence of 'corruption on Earth'.[51]

Being a woman is perilous, but being a woman and an artist is on another level of risk. Widespread censorship and restrictions on who can exhibit or perform are commonplace and for anything to be presented to the public, artists first need authorisation from the Ministry of Culture and Islamic Guidance, something Rezvan's work would never receive.

'Many artists have been forced to pursue their creative freedom by traveling underground (in some cases, quite literally), staging shows in tunnels, caves, homes or isolated fields where officials won't see them, more so as an act of self-preservation rather than of rebellion,' noted Nicole Crowder, in an article for The Washington Post. 'Iranian artists can navigate between the more mainstream and underground scenes as well. For example, it is possible for an artist to take part in an official performance while working on different underground/illegal projects.'[52]

Millions of Iranians have left the country since the revolution in 1979. Some have left voluntarily, and others were forced to leave and apply for asylum due to mounting pressure from the Islamic Republic.

There have been waves of resistance in the country over the last forty years, resulting in increased crackdowns on civil society activists. For example, in 2009, the government ran a major campaign of repression following widespread demonstrations against vote-rigging in the presidential elections at the time, resulting in the election of President Mahmoud Ahmedinejad for a second time. Protesters were targeted by security forces and activists were arrested. Those who were able to leave sought asylum in places like Turkey and Iraqi Kurdistan.[53] By mid-2022, there were 142,346 refugees from Iran and 64,937 asylum-seekers, according to UNHCR data.[54]

Since September 2022 there have been waves of protests in Iran and across the world following the suspicious death of Mahsa Amini during her arrest for not wearing the hijab in accordance with law. Iranian authorities claim she died by heart attack at the police station while eyewitnesses and leaked medical scans show she died following violent attacks to her head by police. Thousands came out to protest the regime with nearly 600 killed and at least 1,160 people injured by April 2023.[55]

Rezvan's work focuses a lot on women's bodies, with photographs of naked skin covered in the writings of Iranian poet Forough Farrokhzad. On one of their night-time dalliances, they painted graffiti that depicted a naked woman with her head removed, guns surrounding her, covered in blood. They would paint on abandoned buildings, walls of houses. Once, they even painted on the outside wall of a masjid.

The last time Rezvan was on that courtyard with her father was in 2015. She had just been accepted to display her work at an exhibition in France called 'Hip-hop: From the Bronx to Arab Countries', at the Institute of the Arab World. Officially, she would be displaying her work on Iranian ceramics and unofficially, her photographs. She packed what she needed for the trip and gave her keys to her parents so they could water her plants while she was away. She thought she would be coming straight back after the exhibition.

After a week with her family, Rezvan travelled to Tehran but she was stressed. Although she had all the approvals she needed to leave Iran and go to France, it was the first time she would leave the country, and the first time she would be taking a plane. She couldn't eat for days before the flight. Like the others we've got to know in their journey towards exile, when she shakily stepped on to the plane, she had no idea she wouldn't be returning.

Just over ten days after she arrived in France, Rezvan called her parents to tell them about what a good time she was having and how well the exhibition was going. Her excitement was squashed when her father said that the government searched the house, going through all her things after finding out what she was really exhibiting in France. If she went back after the raid, she would be arrested on the spot.

'I wasn't prepared at all to stay here in France,' Rezvan told me. 'It was a shock. But if I went back I would go to prison... Just doing graffiti is a crime in Iran. That's why I was very scared.'

She couldn't go back to Iran and had no idea what to do. She didn't speak a word of French and only knew a little bit of English. She didn't know anyone in France, had no family there and no income.

Thankfully, her luck turned when people she had met during her first weeks in France introduced her to an Iranian lawyer who was familiar with her situation. They helped her settle in France and successfully apply for asylum on the basis that she'd be in danger should she return.

To begin her integration into her new home, Rezvan took part in some programs such as Welcome Refugees, organised by Sciences Po University. She also got in touch with Singa, an association that helps integrate refugees into French society. The program put her in touch with a family that offered Rezvan a place to stay in Cachan. At a time when she was forced to separate from her family and the home she grew up in, it helped to be part of this family who welcomed her with open arms.

Today, Rezvan continues to focus on the subject of oppressed women, drawing attention to issues like violence against women. Being in France, she says she can at least work freely. But she is afraid for her family. Still, she wants to help women and tell their stories. Even though she knows her work won't help change Iranian laws or government, she wants to help Iranian women in any way she can. It's her dream to one day return to Iran, her birthplace, her family's home, *her* home. She hopes that the laws will change and would even just be happy to travel there once, without fear of arrest, to see her family. But she says that with her work to give women more freedom, she can never return until the regime falls.

In the meantime, she settles for phone calls with her family who remind her of all the tastes of Iran and the recipes of the food she has forgotten in the years she has been in France.

Chapter 3

A state of terror and confusion

There is an understated, crescent-shaped pastry in Turkey made by combining the cakes that didn't sell by the end of the day and stuffing them inside some dough. It's nothing fancy, and it is definitely not the best-tasting pastry produced in the country, but it was the one that Pinar Ogun suddenly started craving one random day while sitting in her new home in Cardiff.

That pastry became a type of symbol of Pinar's exile after she tweeted about it, with one woman even saying that she would learn how to make it and when her baby boy asked what it was, she would tell him that it was 'Pinar's pastry'. Of course, it wasn't something Pinar could find in Wales.

Sometimes, it's the simplest, most unexpected things

we crave when we are far from home. The commotion of sounds on the street when all the passers-by are speaking your mother tongue, a shitty little pastry that you wouldn't look at twice if you saw it at the patisserie. You understand their worth once you lose them, Pinar says.

She also misses her own identity.

'I miss speaking without having to think about what I'm going to say. When you speak English, you take on a borrowed identity. But when you speak Turkish, you use words and sentences that come with history, that carry meaning because of your experiences. You speak with a lot more nuance and meaning,' she said.

Pinar is still living in Cardiff a decade after she first arrived. At the time, she was so focused on what had just happened to her, what pushed her to leave her home country, that she didn't think far beyond the immediate, understandably. Even waking up and thinking about what she was going to do the next day was stressful. Focus had to be on surviving day to day, figuring out what you need to do in the next five minutes a hundred of times a day.

Pinar had to leave Turkey in a frantic rush. Her and her husband at the time Memet Ali Alabora took part in the Gezi Park protests that started on the 28th of May, 2013 against plans to build a shopping mall and develop the area occupied by a park in Istanbul's Taksim Gezi Park. When police attacked protestors with tear gas and water cannons, the movement to protect the park from demolition turned into wider anti-government demonstrations. Millions across Turkey went out on to the streets to protest the government, led by prime minister Recep Tayyip Erdogan. From May to August, more than eight thousand people were injured and eight people were killed. Around 5,300 people were detained and 160 were arrested. The protests eventually died down and the government's repression of activists increased. Many were prosecuted for trying to overthrow the government by organising or participating in the protests. As Pinar and Memet Ali were among the most high-profile protesters due to their reputation as actors, a large amount of the blame for the protest was focused on them. As the protests were taking place, Pinar and her ex-husband started receiving threats.

The main lawsuit was against philanthropist and human rights activist Osman Kavala and 17 others, including Pinar and her now ex-husband, that lasted over four years. A verdict was reached in 2022, giving Kavala an aggravated life sentence and seven others were sentenced to 18 years in prison. Because Pinar and several other defendants, including journalist Can Dundar were abroad, the prosecutors asked for their case to be separated and held until they could be caught.

It was claimed that these actors, journalists, and architects were part of a conspiracy to overthrow the government and a play that Pinar had put on a year before the protests erupted was highlighted as a dress rehearsal for it. Pro-government papers were writing articles about these public figures, claiming that nothing was a coincidence. One such piece was published by daily Yeni Safak: 'Information revealed that the Gezi protests, which turned into a civil coup attempt, were fictionalized: The rehearsal of the protests took place for months in the play 'Mi Minor' staged in Istanbul with the support of a UK-based agency.'[56]

Pinar's ex-husband was put under the protection of the gendarmerie, ordered by the President at the time, Abdullah Gul. They were watched every day, essentially living under confinement for their own protection. However, despite this surveillance, when Pinar found a note left on her car, parked right outside her house, saying that she would die, she knew she had to leave Turkey, and quickly.

The frantic rush out of Turkey began as she left the house for the airport that evening with some cash, leaving her ex-husband behind with the protection. She first travelled to Amsterdam and then London. From London, she took a train to Cardiff, where she would eventually establish her new home.

Pinar says that sometimes, the lies that people tell about you can make you question your own mind. That's how she felt at one point, reading all the conspiracy theories about herself, from how she apparently helped organise the 2013 protests against President Erdogan, who was Prime Minister at the time, to how she was trained as an MI6 agent and part of a conspiracy dating back to the Battle of Malazgirt, fought in 1071 between the Byzantine Empire and the Seljuk Empire.

She had studied in London between 2006 and 2008, which for some was proof enough that she was trained by MI6. She also had a role in a film called *Closed Circuit* that was released at the same time as the protests. In this film she played the wife of a man, whose last name was Erdogan and who was suspected of detonating a bomb in London. This was seen as further proof of her being a foreign agent and her character's last name was a subtle defamation of the Turkish Prime Minister.

Her previous work in a TV show dramatising the life of Turkan Saylan, a doctor, social activist and academic, didn't help. Saylan, a champion of women's rights, herself became the target of a probe into an alleged conspiracy to overthrow the government in 2009. Her house was searched, and her files confiscated. Shortly after, following a long battle with cancer, Saylan passed away.

'There was a time when being secular, laic, was normal in Turkey. But at the time of this TV show, being secular started becoming a problem,' Pinar said. So, the dots were connected, and she was branded a foreign agent.

Before Memet Ali joined her a month following her

departure, Pinar first stayed at a hotel in Cardiff. That same week there was a Bruce Springsteen concert in town, which meant that it was the busiest it had been, with people filling the streets, drinking, having raucous fun.

'I can't tell you the paralysing fear that I felt. I couldn't understand anything, walking around like a headless chicken. Your dreams become weird; you get confused. One moment you're laughing and the next you're crying. I was in a very different mindset. The consequences of what they had been saying about me was me leaving the country with the fear of being killed. There was no physical threat like a gun pointed at my head, but I received so much cyber bullying and death threats. When I arrived, I couldn't speak English from fear. There were people outside partying, and I had just left such an extreme situation that you don't feel like you're living in the same reality,' she explained.

Getting familiar with a new bureaucratic system is also one of the most difficult things for a person in exile, in her opinion. All the necessary documents, how to rent a new home, what references you need, it can feel endless. As she was in hiding in Cardiff, she couldn't use her credit card and had disposed of her phone, which makes it very difficult to find flat in the UK as proof of income and contact information is essential for the renting process. To provide income, you need a bank account.

To get a bank account, you need a phone number. To get a phone number, you need proof of address... on and on. Without external help, the whole process becomes extremely frustrating and impossible.

'I got a phone and a new SIM card, but I couldn't call anyone in Turkey because I was worried they might get into trouble. You need to think how they would think, so you cannot do anything because you're afraid that people close to you might get hurt,' she said.

Since she left Istanbul in 2013, she was able to go back just once to visit her family, in 2015. Less than a year later, Turkey was rocked with a coup attempt. Her being in the country prior to the coup attempt did not do her any favours in the eyes of her detractors. She was back to being a prominent part of conspiracy theories. She hasn't been back since.

But she did manage to eat the pastry again, with her friends sending some from Turkey.

Although Turkey is one of the largest host countries for refugees, with nearly 4 million Syrians currently in the country, there are also many asylum-seekers from Turkey who have been forced to leave the country due to fear of persecution. Since being elected Prime Minister in 2003 and subsequently becoming President in 2014, Erdogan has increasingly rolled back human rights and targeted dissidents and opponents for punishment.

Since the attempted coup in 2016, opponents of

Erdogan have faced increasing persecution. The failed coup was used by Erdogan to initiate a widespread crackdown, which in the first few months led to the arrest of more than 40,000 people, including dozens of academics, and over 100,000 people were sacked from state institutions.[57] In 2019, Turkish asylum seekers were the third-most registered group in Germany, after Syrians and Iraqis, according to BAMF.[58] In the first nine months of 2022, there was a 254% increase in the number of Turkish refugees arriving in Germany.[59] There has also been an unprecedented number of Turks crossing the border to the US from Mexico to seek asylum. A total of 31,485 Turks entered the US through this route since 2020, seeking asylum because of discrimination in Turkey due to their political beliefs, religion or gender.[60]

New laws, such as one on disinformation, have been adopted, creating new avenues for the government to crackdown on freedom of expression. The disinformation law[61] ratified in 2022, for example, includes a jail sentence of up to three years for those accused of spreading disinformation. Critics say, however, that it provides a framework for censorship and criminalisation of journalism.

Currently, it doesn't look like there will be an end to the exodus from Turkey any time soon. The presidential election held in May 2023 saw Erdogan re-elected, while his political party, in partnership with the nationalist MHP party, once again won majority in the parliament. Opponents of the government have been concerned that this will mean the further erosion of rights in Turkey, and many are already looking to leave. Thousands have already sought to leave, with Turkey moving up to third place for asylum applications to the EU last year.[62] According to UNHCR, by mid-2022 there were 51,444 asylum-seekers from Turkey, up from 46,327 in 2021.[63] Turks lodged 6,400 applications for asylum in January 2023, more than a third above the 2022 monthly average.[64]

Pinar was able to settle in the UK easily – a fate not shared by many people arriving in the country after escaping war or persecution.

The Tory government in power at the time of writing has been working to curb what it deems illegal immigration and deter people from seeking asylum.

One of the big complaints they have is that those who are crossing into the UK by boat with no appropriate documentation are entering the country illegally and should come via legal routes. However, it is not possible to claim asylum from outside the UK, except for a handful of special schemes such as ones arranged for Afghans and Ukrainians in the face of their respective wars. These were set up as emergency measures following

Russia's invasion of Ukraine and the Taliban takeover of Afghanistan as the people from these countries faced immediate danger.

But these schemes are not as straightforward as they should be. In 2022 the UK government promised to take up to 20,000 people from Afghanistan, who were fleeing the Taliban, including up to 5,000 in the first year.[65] However, according to the Refugee Council, only 22 Afghans were resettled in the UK in the year since January 2022 under Pathway 2 of the scheme, which is the only route open for Afghans who are not already in the UK.[66] There is also no UK visa for people to enter 'legally' to claim asylum, therefore most have no choice but to enter the UK first, without permission, and then claim asylum.[67] This has become even more difficult since the introduction of the Nationality and Borders Act of 2022. Under this law, anyone entering the UK without a visa and claiming asylum can face a sentence of four years. Those who re-renter the UK after a deportation order face five years in prison.

At present in 2023, if you wanted to find a way to enter the UK with a valid visa but with the intention of applying for asylum once you are in the country, this would only be possible if you lied in your visa application. If you're on a tourist visa and apply for asylum, you can be accused of deception and your request would most likely be denied.

Although the government likes to paint a picture of 'illegal migrants' arriving in the UK and then just disappearing into the system to drain the UK's resources, without applying for any kind of protection, the numbers tell a different story. The Home Office's own numbers show that in 2022, 90% of 44,666 small boat arrivals claimed asylum[68] and at least 60% of these will be recognised as refugees – meaning their claims are deemed legitimate.[69] Yet, the Conservative government has made it its mission to restrict migration across the UK and has targeted refugees and asylum-seekers. The government unveiled the Illegal Migration Bill in March 2023 to stop small boats arriving on its shores. Under the bill, those arriving illegally in the UK are to be removed either back to their own country or to Rwanda, which the UK government has deemed safe, contrary to international opinion. The other main clause in the bill states that the UK will deny lawful immigration status or access to the asylum system to anyone who enters the country illegally. They will never be allowed back into the UK, even if they are a genuine refugee. The problems with this are numerous but one irony exists in the taxpayer cost, which the Conservative government insists will be eased by fewer immigrants. However, the Refugee Council identified that the proposals 'to remove the right to claim asylum from those crossing on boats would lead to thousands of people living in limbo and potentially being locked up in detention at huge cost of hundreds of millions of pounds to the taxpayer'.[70]

While the UK has welcomed Pinar its doors are increasingly being shut to many asylum seekers.

Chapter 4
Waiting to return

Escape from Ukraine

As Russia launched its full-scale attack on Ukraine on the 24th of February, 2022, Sasha Morozova was home, in Kyiv, playing the piano. Although she was scared by the threats outside, she focused on her music, not knowing what else to do. She had ten missed calls from a friend inviting Sasha to her house just outside of the city. She tried to call a taxi before but to no avail. When she tried an Uber this time round, she wasn't expecting one to be only minutes away. She had eight minutes to pack up her bag, grab her dog and take the taxi to her friend's house. She thought she would be going back home soon enough, so didn't pack much.

'I took what I could with me in those eight minutes, and I haven't been back to my flat since,' she recalled. She only took a hoodie and some leggings with her, in addition to some food for the dog and her passport. At the time, her mother was living in Hostomel, the city that became one of the first targets of Russian occupiers. The town was occupied for 35 days until it was liberated on the 2nd of April, 2022. It's thought that more than 400 people went missing in the town during the occupation.[71] Sasha's mother was living under the Russian occupation during that time with constant bombing.

Part of the city was destroyed and there was no electricity, gas or water. Her mother was living above a little shop and was lucky that the owner told the residents in the building to go there and take whatever they needed. That's how they survived during the occupation.

But for at least ten days, Sasha heard nothing from her mother. When she arrived at her friend's house with her dog, she tried to find out any news she could, afraid that she had died. All they could do was wait. Her friend had three of her children with her and another dog. 'The first time with my friend when we decided we will wait, we didn't know if it was going to be our last days, we bought some champagne and celebrated life. We played the piano. We can't be depressed all the time. You need to survive and your brain finds a way,' Sasha explained. 'Every day there were sirens and bombings, but they had a piano. While everyone ran underground, I would just play the piano. If it was going to be my last minutes, at least I was playing music.'

One day, her friend managed to find some petrol and decided that it was time for them to leave. She had to get her children out. They took the car and drove West. It took them about five hours to go 100km because of the traffic, as everyone seemed to have the same idea. Sasha split from the group after that as they decided to go to different borders, with Sasha aiming for Poland.

'When war happens, you don't think too much. When we decided to run, my friend was focused on saving her children. And me, I needed to save me, my mom, my dog. You just do things automatically. You just need to find a way. You don't have so many feelings, because you need to find a way.' But she still didn't have news from her mother and was reluctant to leave Ukraine without her.

She arranged to meet with a friend of hers who lived in France but was driving to the Polish border and found a man to drive her there. It took them around nine hours to cross the border, after which they found a hotel. This was when Russia agreed to establish evacuation corridors so civilians could flee. Sasha was incredibly surprised and happy when she received a call from her mother. Sasha told her mother to run and meet her at the Polish border.

This time she contacted another friend who was in Poland, who could come help her. He picked her up to drive back to the border to pick up her mother and take them to Lublin. 'He found a hotel, paid for it and organised everything. We spent some days there and decided what to do next,' Sasha said.

At this time Sasha was speaking to a film director she knew, Andrew Tkach. She previously appeared in one of his films, *Generation Maidan: A Year of Revolution and War*, where he interviewed various people from medics to musicians on the 2014 Revolution of Dignity in Ukraine, which led to the removal of the President. Andrew lived in Messery in France and invited Sasha and her mother to stay with him. They arrived in the country on the 17th of March. Andrew helped her with the formalities to stay in France.

After settling from the long, stressful journey, Sasha went to Paris to play in a charity concert for Ukraine. 'I was here twenty years ago with my teacher for the first time, when we attended a classical music competition. We visited museums and went to Musee D'Orsay to see impressionist painters. I had forgotten how beautiful this city is. When I came back I decided I want to move back here and find something here,' she said. This time around though, there were no museum visits and no enjoying the tourist life. 'You're a refugee so it's a totally different feeling,' she said. 'You are safe, there are no bombs, no sirens, but you check the news every day and many of my friends are still in Kyiv.'

After enduring weeks of bombing and the Russian occupation in Hostomel, Sasha knew her mother needed some peace and quiet. In the end, she managed to find a place in Annecy and settled her there with her dog. Sasha decided that she would move to Paris. She didn't want to just be a refugee, though. She wanted to showcase her culture, help Ukraine with her music and bring people's attention to the atrocities happening. 'So many people lose their homes. I never thought that I could leave all my life so easily,' she said. 'But you just do it because you have to. You're not worried about anything, just finding a safe place.'

Since 2014, when Russia annexed Crimea, millions of Ukrainians have been displaced from their homes. Before the full-scale invasion in 2022, an estimated 1.4 million people had left their homes.[72] Now, more than a year on since Russia invaded Ukraine, more than 13 million have been displaced, including nearly eight million refugees across Europe.[73] According to a UNHCR survey, the vast majority of Ukrainian refugees, some 77%, want to return home one day, but safety and security concerns are preventing them.[74]

The majority of Ukrainians who have left the country have sought asylum in neighbouring countries, particularly Poland, Czech Republic and Germany. As the war in Ukraine continues at the time of writing, the number of refugees is likely to increase.

When Sasha first arrived in France, it was a strange experience, a polar opposite of her last few weeks in

Ukraine, with France's peace and beautiful nature. 'You check the news, you feel you're not good enough, because you don't do anything, you just run away and many people still died. You don't know how to help. You don't care about your things, I don't know if I go back to Ukraine, will I still have a home or not. But I don't think about it. Because the big problem is to save lives and people as much as possible.'

She was surprised that so many people were willing to help and how many nice people she met while in France. But it's difficult making long term plans. 'After the 24th of February, I have no plans. Because I had some plans before, now I just try to feel and find my way. As you can see, it's a dangerous time and I don't want to leave my mother in a city that's being bombed. If I go back, my mother will as well. Sometimes I think maybe I should go back and help somehow. But I'm not sure it's a good idea.'

Sasha talks about the importance of having a community as an artist, no matter where you are. Born in the USSR, she still remembers her education from that period, made up of propaganda. But the younger generation of artists in Ukraine don't remember the USSR and are creating a brand new culture. Mixing with artists of different backgrounds and history was something Sasha always cherished when she was in Ukraine. She felt that she could create art with them and share experiences. She misses her community.

In Paris, Sasha has joined the Agency of Artists in Exile that now help her organise concerts and connect artists from different backgrounds and they have become her new family. But since the start of the invasion, even since the Russian annexation of Crimea, Sasha says her music has changed.

She describes her music before as being softer, more ethereal, as though a person is slowly swimming or dancing. But now, it is not as relaxed. She knows exactly where she wants to go with the notes on the piano and she gets there without any detours.

'Before, I could dream about something. Now, I have to be exact, strict, with purpose. Our army is very good, they are very strict and I just feel like I have to be the same. I need to practice my skills and do my job very well, not dream about something. Before, it was more horizontal, I had a lot of waves in my music. And now it's more vertical and strict. More disciplined.'

To stay or go

As Anastasiia Prigoda made sure she had all her necessary documents with her before she left for the airport, she knew she only had two options. She could stay in Russia but she wouldn't be able to live as she wanted due to the discrimination against LGBT+ people in the country, or she could leave her home but at least she wouldn't be afraid of being herself.

It was the 21st of September, 2021. She felt that it was her last chance to escape Russia. She was living with her mother and her dog at the time in the Republic of Adygea, in the North Caucasus, where one-fourth of the population is Muslim. Anastasiia was born there and lived in the area for 17 years. She prepared her documents and printed out her plane ticket but was worried.

She had a Schengen visa from Finland so she could enter the EU, but it was following the COVID-19 outbreak and she only had the Russian Sputnik vaccine, which wasn't certified in Europe. She said she was in a state of shock and stress as she was worried that she would be told to go back to Russia once she landed in Spain.

'It was so stressful because I bought the ticket even though I didn't have a lot of money and was worried they can return me to my country. I knew it was my last chance to escape this country,' she told me over a video call. 'At this time, we had a lot of problems with gay rights, especially lesbian and women's rights because we have the Muslim traditions in this part of Russia. And if you're a woman you didn't have anything, no equality and no rights.'

Still, in her mind she was only escaping for a little while. She had every intention to go back to Russia. She had been working as a lawyer with advocacy group

Coming Out and fighting for the rights of LGBT+ people in the country. That was her calling and she intended to continue.

Her first flight was to Greece and then to Madrid in Spain. She was going to first study Spanish, as she didn't know the language at all, and then she was hoping to do a master's degree in human rights law. Four months into her stay in Spain, Russia invaded Ukraine. President Vladimir Putin also passed a new law prohibiting LGBT+ propaganda.[75] On top of it all, the organisation she worked for, Coming Out, was designated as a 'foreign agent', prohibited in Russia.

That's when she knew she couldn't go back.

Half her family lives in Ukraine, in Mariupol, one of the most heavily bombarded cities during the war. They have now moved to Dnipro, although they haven't escaped the constant shelling from Russia. 'I'm Ukrainian with a Russian passport. I'm a lesbian, LGBT+ activist from the North Caucasus and I'm a lawyer. My existence was dangerous for the state,' she explained. 'If I return they will kill me,' she thought. She was only 23 years old at the time.

She knew that there was a law against LGBT+ people in the works, but she thought they could fight against it. She thought if she received her master's degree in Spain, she could return and fight for LGBT+ and women's rights.

In Russia, there has long been a history of hostility towards LGBT+ people. Anastasiia says after she came out to her parents, around the time she was 12 years old, it became dangerous for her to walk in the street or go to school. She experienced this first hand while in school, when one of her classmates attacked her. You can still see the scars on her arm. 'I thought the world is a cruel place and you cannot live in this world if you're an LGBT+ person and you're a woman,' she recalled.

When she moved to St. Petersburg for her studies – once the gay capital of Russia – she thought things would be different. She thought it would be her escape from the Muslim community she grew up in. But she faced discrimination even from her professors at university once they understood she was gay. They told her that LGBT+ people were people who had mental problems and that they should stay in prison or be put in hospitals. 'I was in shock and I had situations where I was physically attacked on the street,' she told me. Although she reported it to the police nothing happened.

Although Anastasiia worked as a lawyer for several years in Russia, helping the LGBT+ community, with the new laws against them and the rise in conversion therapy around the country, she feels her work was all for nothing.

She now lives in Valencia but she is afraid. Her mother once received a call from the FSB – the Russian intelligence services – asking her about Anastasiia, where she is and when she will return. Since then, the FSB has interviewed her mother several times. They showed her mother that they had been tracking her in Valencia, showing pictures of her there. 'They know everything about me and exactly where I live,' she said. 'They understand that I'm an activist and they hate people like me. For them I'm the biggest threat and they use this against my family.'

She is also afraid in Spain because of her status. She is waiting for the approval of her refugee status but because of the uncertainty of who Spain's next leader will be after parties failed to gain an outright majority in elections in July 2023, she doesn't know what will happen, particularly if right-wing parties come out on top.

Spain was third among EU countries to receive asylum seekers in 2022. But only 16.5% of the 118,842 applications were approved, compared with the EU's average of 38.5% according to the Spanish Commission for Refugees (CEAR).[76] The organisation criticised the country's lack of safe and legal pathways to asylum.[77] It also pointed out that lengthy bureaucracy and a dysfunctional appointment system means that thousands of people cannot request asylum. More than 122,000 files are still awaiting resolution, with the majority of people waiting for months and even years.[78]

As in other countries, right wing politicians in Spain also use immigration as a critical issue to gain support.

While July 2023 elections led to extreme right wing party Vox losing many seats in the parliament, its anti-immigrant stance has still contributed to the rise of negative attitudes towards immigration in the country.[79]

Anastasiia initially chose Spain as her destination because when she visited the country as a tourist as a 19-year-old, it was the first time she saw an LGBT+ flag in public. 'When I saw the flag in the street, I thought *How is this possible?* I studied in St. Petersburg, it's the second biggest city in Russia and officially eight million people live there. 20 years ago, it was the gay capital of Russia but it's impossible to imagine an LGBT+ flag in the street. When I saw it in Spain, I understood the world is different. You don't need to suffer all your life,' she explained.

But she has also experienced discrimination in Spain and the rest of Europe. This time not because of her sexual orientation but because of her nationality. Although she is Ukrainian and is adamantly against the war, when people find out she's Russian, they have acted as though all Russians side with Putin. Anastasiia was working on obtaining a master's degree from a university in Germany from a distance. As the war against Ukraine unfolded, the university rescinded her place on her course. Although they didn't say it was because she was Russian, she believes that was the reason. While attending a COVID vaccination appointment, the doctor saw her passport and told her that she should go back to her country and fight. She also told Anastasiia that she should go to another hospital because they couldn't help her.

All of this combined makes it difficult to feel at home. 'I have international protection. Because of this I feel safe. But on the other hand, it's not my home because I lost my home. I had a home in Ukraine, in Mariupol and I lost that too. I lost my two homes and sometimes I think I should build a new one for my future.'

Conclusion

Living in exile carries different meanings for different people. It impacts identities and the sense of self in a myriad of ways. It can be both traumatic and transformative.

While one person finds that they can make a new home in their host country and adapt to a new life easily, for another, the state will always remain temporary until the day they can return, although that day may never come.

In a recent interview with We Are Europe, Judith Depaule, director of L'Atelier des artistes en exil (Agency of Artists in Exile) in France – an organisation several of the interviewees are a part of – provides the following explanation which is worth quoting in full:

> …you can't imagine what it means to leave everything behind, to leave home. You will never be *at home* here. You can feel comfortable in a country that is not your own, but it will never be your *home*.

Everything will push us, everything will make us understand that this is not *home*.

Exile is a delicate balance between loss and gain. The loss of home, of your previous life, of your loved ones, of your reference points. The gain of this new world where you are enriched by other things, where you learn other things, where you meet other people, where you have other opportunities. It's a constant back and forth between this loss and this gain.

There is also the choice to live with nostalgia or not, to stay in community or not.

You have to think about the boomerang of exile, which is expressed in post-traumatic syndromes, episodes of decompensation and various illnesses. Exile affects minds and bodies. The temporality of this shock wave is personal. Some people arrive and are completely apathetic and depressed, others will show this type of behaviour three or four years afterwards, it is impossible to predict.

Perhaps there is something in their integration that will hurt them terribly and make them go back to square one.[80]

According to Dr. Lijtmaer the feeling of homelessness is an 'emotional self-state' and continuous contact with a new culture leads to the transformation of internal structures and internalised object relations.[81]

In the case of people in exile, particularly of asylum seekers, there are usually socio-political traumatic events involved where they usually leave in a hectic rush and, in some cases, their families back home still face danger that the refugee has (possibly only temporarily) escaped.

'They do not have time to mourn their losses, there is no time for pleasantries or "ideal migration" where destination countries can choose who they will take in. Refugees suffer rejection, endure dehumanisation and shame in addition to feelings of helplessness, loss of dignity, frustration, and anger since nobody wants them. Their initial hopes and dreams of escaping to a safe "haven" are transformed into nightmares of humiliation and fear. Many of these asylum seekers are now, or will soon be, suffering from PTSD, due to massive psychic trauma. Such a traumatic assault often leads to the loss of physical cohesion and continuity of the self.'[82]

The loss of one's homeland, community, and cultural identity can lead to a sense of displacement, isolation, and grief. The psychological impact of exile can manifest in various forms, such as depression, anxiety, PTSD, and a range of physical health problems. Meanwhile, the lack of social support, economic opportunities, and legal rights can exacerbate the challenges of adapting to a new environment.

There is also the uncertainty to deal with. Not just as it relates to whether the person in exile will ever be able to return to their home country but also generally what the future will look like for them. Because going into exile is so out of the ordinary that you cannot plan for it and envision a future where you are living in exile. There is also the uncertainty of how you will be received in your host country.

The uncertainty associated with conflict and exile can create feelings of insecurity and fear, of ambiguity and contradiction, of psychological stress.[83]

Despite these difficulties, however, some exiles have found ways to adapt and thrive. They may form new social connections, build new skills, and develop a sense of resilience that enables them to cope with the ongoing challenges of exile.

After the initial reaction, the immigration experience can build character and resilience, according to Lijtmaer, and can be a 'process of new possibilities and of a hopeful future'.[84] This is what we can observe in many of the stories, with Taha for example, finding a new home in France, hopeful for the future.

Other stories, like Sasha's, gives us a glimpse of the guilt one can feel while living in exile. Guilt over not returning to fight to make things better in one's home country. But that also creates an ambition. An ambition to do whatever one can to help from abroad, as Sasha tries to do with her music.

Meanwhile, Pinar's experience shows how lies and

conspiracy theories can impact a person's life and their experience of going into exile.

Conspiracy theories have sadly become commonplace and lies about activists and their critics are one of the most widely used tools in the arsenal of oppressive governments. So much so that it can silence opponents and even drive them away to seek safety in another country. But the psychological impact of being the subject of such lies, putting a target on a person's back are rarely discussed in the media.

Running away from death threats, exacerbated by lies being told about you can be traumatising. One study on the psychological effects of exile describes it as 'one of the most challenging experiences in life'.[85] Researchers noted, 'Beyond the heavy burden of all vital difficulties and limitations caused by the exile event, the constant feeling of homelessness, inaccessibility of the motherland, and the vitality of memories, the losses during exile have a shocking effect on the individuals.'[86]

On top of this, death threats are seen as powerful stressors for individuals. A *Vice* article once described death threats as 'tossing a bomb into another person's mind.'[87] That state of shock is how Pinar felt, running away from death threats following the lies being published about her by pro-government media and social media trolls. Being hunted, the subject of constant attack, and getting blamed for implausible actions have a deep impact on psychology – to the point where the subject begins questioning their own actions. Insecurity is then not just physically manifest, but it's internalised, something impossible to shake off, no matter how much a new country becomes a new 'home'.

Unfortunately, the experiences recounted in this book are just a handful among millions of cases of displacement. At the end of 2021, there were 89.3 million forcibly displaced people worldwide.[88] Of these, 27.1 million were refugees, 53.2 million were internally displaced people, and 4.6 million were asylum seekers. The majority of these people, some 83%, were hosted in low and middle-income countries, with Turkey hosting (officially) nearly 4 million, making up the largest population of refugees worldwide.[89] More than two thirds of refugees came from five countries: Syria, Venezuela, Afghanistan, South Sudan and Myanmar. Children account for 41% of all forcibly displaced people.[90]

'Every year of the last decade, the numbers have climbed,' noted Filippo Grandi, UN High Commissioner for Refugees. 'Either the international community comes together to take action to address this human tragedy, resolve conflicts and find lasting solutions, or this terrible trend will continue.'[91] The International Crisis Group tracks more than 70 conflicts and crises worldwide, from Israel-Palestine and Tunis to Sri Lanka and Indonesia.

In 2021, 23 countries, with a total population of 850 million people, faced high or medium-intensity conflicts, according to the World Bank. In the last decade, this number has doubled.[92]

According to the European Union Agency for Asylum in the second half of 2022 and in early 2023, there was a major increase in applications for international protection in the EU.[93] They have been at the highest levels since the so-called 2015-16 refugee crisis – although the figures do not include the several million Ukrainians who have registered for temporary protection.[94]

There are different routes to reach safety and some who take these paths are luckier than others. According to the Missing Migrants Project, there have been more than 26,200 deaths during migration in the Mediterranean since 2014.[95] In Africa there have been 12,566, in Asia 7,652, in the Americas 7,667 and in Europe 985.[96]

Governmental pushback of migrants and asylum seekers across Europe, and the criminalisation of search and rescue operations have only helped to increase these numbers. No matter how people arrive in a new country, whether via dangerous routes at sea, to then be demonised by politicians, or via flying in after escaping death threats and kidnapping attempts, refugees and asylum seekers increasingly face hostile systems, prolonged uncertainty and negative perceptions as well as their own internal turmoil and questions around identity as they often move from one side of a continent to another, with no safety net or 'home' awaiting them.

On top of it all, the experience of living in exile can have a profound impact on an individual's mental health, but it can also present opportunities for personal growth and resilience. While the stories of people living in exile remind us of this resilience of the human spirit, they also express the importance of providing support and assistance to those who have been forced to leave their homes and communities.

References

1   "Alan Kurdi's Story: Behind the Most Heartbreaking Photo
    of 2015." Bryan Walsh, *Time*, 29 December 2015. time.
    com/4162306/alan-kurdi-syria-drowned-boy-refugee-crisis/.
    Accessed 16 October 2023.
2   Ibid.
3   "Alarmist rhetoric about 'mass immigration' paints a picture
    out of step with reality." Abdeslam Marfouk, *Equal Times*,
    20 April 2023. equaltimes.org/alarmist-rhetoric-about-mass.
    Accessed 14 July 2023.
4   Abdeslam Marfouk (2019) I'm neither racist nor xenophobic,
    but: dissecting European attitudes towards a ban on Muslims'
    immigration, Ethnic and Racial Studies, 42:10, 1747-1765,
    DOI: 10.1080/01419870.2018.1519585
5   Ibid.
6   "Suella Braverman calls 'broken' immigration system an 'inva-
    sion on south coast'". *The Independent*, YouTube, 31 October
    2022.youtube.com/watch?v=hG-E8GwWjYc. Accessed 16
    October 2023.
7   "UK Home Secretary Suella Braverman says it's her "dream"
    to see asylum seekers sent to Rwanda" *Middle East Eye*, You-
    Tube, 2 October 2022. youtube.com/watch?v=cZqYxJuA-8o.
    Accessed 14 July 2023.
8   "France looks to crack down on illegal immigration with
    new law." *RFI*, 6 December 2022. rfi.fr/en/france/20221206-

france-looks-to-crack-down-on-illegal-immigration-with-new-law. Accessed 16 October 2023.

9   "What's in the French government's new immigration bill?" Julia Pascual, *Le Monde*, 1 February 2023. lemonde.fr/en/france/article/2023/02/01/what-s-in-the-french-government-s-new-immigration-bill_6014005_7.html. Accessed 16 October 2023.

10 Ibid.

11 "When refugee displacement drags on, is self-reliance the answer?" Elizabeth Ferris, *Brookings*, 19 June 2018. brookings.edu/articles/when-refugee-displacement-drags-on-is-self-reliance-the-answer/. Accessed 13 July 2023.

12 "Mental health and forced displacement." *World Health Organization*, 31 August 2021. who.int/news-room/fact-sheets/detail/mental-health-and-forced-displacement. Accessed 16 October 2023.

13 Ibid.

14 Lijtmaer, Ruth. (2022). Social Trauma, Nostalgia and Mourning in the Immigration Experience. The American Journal of Psychoanalysis. 82. 10.1057/s11231-022-09357-8. Accessed 28 March 2023.

15 "RSF's 2022 World Press Freedom Index: a new era of polarisation." *Reporters Without Borders*. rsf.org/en/rsf-s-2022-world-press-freedom-index-new-era-polarisation. Accessed 16 October 2023.

16 "At least 42 journalists killed in Pakistan during last four years." *The Express Tribune*, 20 January 2023. tribune.com.pk/story/2396964/at-least-42-journalists-killed-in-pakistan-during-last-four-years. Accessed 16 October 2023.

17 "Your lives are in danger, police warn Pakistani dissidents in UK." Mark Townsend, Kiyya Baloch, *The Guardian*, 5 February 2022. theguardian.com/world/2022/feb/05/your-lives-are-in-danger-police-warn-pakistani-dissidents-in-uk. Accessed 16 October 2023.

18 Ibid.

19 Ibid.

20 "UNHCR - Refugee Statistics." *UNHCR*. unhcr.org/refugee-statistics/download/?url=2bxU2f. Accessed 16 October 2023.

21 "Where's the 'bread, freedom and social justice' a year after Egypt's revolution?" Mariz Tadros, The Guardian, 25 January 2012. theguardian.com/global-development/poverty-matters/2012/jan/25/egypt-bread-freedom-social-justice. Accessed 16 October 2023.

22 "Trump's Israel-Palestine 'deal' has always been a fraud." David Dardner, *Financial Times*, 11 June 2019. ft.com/content/f56a9b7e-8c3b-11e9-a24d-b42f641eca37. Accessed 16 October 2023.

23 "Egypt: Dissidents Abroad Denied Identity Documents." *Human Rights Watch*, 13 March 2023. hrw.org/news/2023/03/13/egypt-dissidents-abroad-denied-identity-documents. Accessed 16 October 2023.

24 "Tough choices for Afghan refugees returning home after years in exile." *UNHCR*, 3 February 2017. unhcr.org/news/briefing/2017/2/589453557/tough-choices-afghan-refugees-returning-home-years-exile.html. Accessed 1 April 2023.

25 "Afghanistan situation." *UNHCR*. reporting.unhcr.org/operational/situations/afghanistan-situation. Accessed 16 October 2023.

26 "Latest Asylum Trends." *EUAA*. euaa.europa.eu/latest-asylum-trends-asylum. Accessed 17 March 2023.

27 "AFGHANISTAN HUMANITARIAN CRISIS." *UNHCR*. unrefugees.org/emergencies/afghanistan/. Accessed 17 June 2023.

28 "U.S. is rejecting over 90% of Afghans seeking to enter the country on humanitarian grounds." Camilo Montoya-Galvez, *CBS News*, 20 June 2022. cbsnews.com/news/afghan-refugees-rejected-us-entry-humanitarian-grounds/. Accessed 16 October 2023.

29 "Afghan People Seeking Asylum File Federal Lawsuit Challenging Government Adjudication Delays." *National*

Immigrant Justice Center, 20 April 2023. immigrantjustice.
org/press-releases/afghan-people-seeking-asylum-file-feder-
al-lawsuit-challenging-government. Accessed 13 July 2023.

30   "What is President Biden's 'asylum ban' and what does it
mean for people seeking safety?" *Rescue*, 22 March 2023.
rescue.org/article/what-president-bidens-proposed-asylum-
ban-and-what-does-it-mean-people-seeking-safety. Accessed
16 October 2023.

31   "Biden to replace Trump migration policy with Trump-esque asylum policy" Myah Ward, *Politico*, 21 February 2023.
politico.com/news/2023/02/21/biden-trump-migration-poli-
cy-asylum-00083873. Accessed 16 October 2023.

32   "Florida GOP passes sweeping anti-immigration bill that
gives DeSantis $12 million for migrant transports." Gary Fin-
eout, *Politico*, 2 May 2023. politico.com/news/2023/05/02/
desantis-anti-immigration-florida-00095012. Accessed 16
October 2023.

33   "DeSantis pitches crackdown on illegal immigration in first
major policy proposal of his campaign." Steve Contorno, Kit
Maher, *CNN*, 26 June 2023. edition.cnn.com/2023/06/26/
politics/desantis-immigration-proposal/index.html. Accessed
13 July 2023.

34   Ibid.

35   "Greg Abbott Makes Los Angeles the Latest Backdrop of His
Anti-migrant Stunt Show." Caleb Ecarma, *Vanity Fair*, 15
June 2023. vanityfair.com/news/2023/06/greg-abbott-los-
angeles-latest-backdrop-anti-migrant-stunt. Accessed 13 July
2023.

36   Ibid.

37   "Uniting for Ukraine." *Department of Homeland Security*. dhs.
gov/ukraine. Accessed 16 October 2023.

38   "Biden Administration Ends Humanitarian Parole for Afghan
Refugees." Elizabeth Hagearty, *Boundless*, 6 September 2022,
boundless.com/blog/afghan-refugees-parole-suspended/.
Accessed 13 July 2023.

39   Ibid.

40   The name has been changed to protect his identity.

41   It's only in recent history that asylum seekers can be granted asylum in the European Union based on their sexuality, following a decision by the European Court of Justice in 2013. But applying for asylum as an LGBT+ person in France and the rest of Europe is not as easy as it might be hoped. To be granted asylum under these conditions, the applicant must prove that they are gay, lesbian or queer, and that their fear of persecution in their home country due to their sexuality is well-founded.

42   "Country Report: Spain." Teresa De Gasperis, *Asylum Information Database*, April 2023. asylumineurope.org/wp-content/uploads/2023/04/AIDA-ES_2022update_final.pdf. Accessed 16 October 2023.

43   "UNHCR - Refugee Statistics." *UNHCR*. unhcr.org/refugee-statistics/download/?url=2bxU2f.

44   "Texts Adopted." European Parliament, 19 January 2023. europarl.europa.eu/doceo/document/TA-9-2023-0014_EN.html. Accessed 11 April 2023.

45   "'They'll Get You No Matter What' Morocco's Playbook to Crush Dissent." *Human Rights Watch*, 28 July 2022. hrw.org/report/2022/07/28/theyll-get-you-no-matter-what/moroccos-playbook-crush-dissent. Accessed 16 October 2023.

46   "Morocco: Situation of sexual minorities, including treatment by the authorities and society; the application of Article 489 of the Penal Code and cases with convictions for homosexuality; state protection and support services (2010-October 2013)" refworld.org/docid/53732cbf4.html. Accessed 16 October 2023.

47   "Map of Countries that Criminalise LGBT People." *Human Dignity Trust*, 2023. humandignitytrust.org/lgbt-the-law/map-of-criminalisation/. Accessed 16 October 2023.

48   Ibid.

49   "LGBT asylum seekers' claims routinely rejected in Europe

and UK." Jon Henley, *The Guardian*, 9 July 2020. theguardian.com/uk-news/2020/jul/09/lgbt-asylum-seekers-routinely-see-claims-rejected-in-europe-and-uk. Accessed 16 October 2023.

50 "LGBT people nearly four times more likely than non-LGBT people to be victims of violent crime." *Williams Institute*, 2 October 2020. williamsinstitute.law.ucla.edu/press/ncvs-lgbt-violence-press-release/. Accessed 16 October 2023.

51 "Iran protests: 15 minutes to defend yourself against the death penalty." Maryam Afshang, *BBC News*, 18 January 2023. bbc.com/news/world-middle-east-64302726. Accessed 16 October 2023.

52 "Most art forms in Iran are heavily censored. So many artists chose to perform underground." Nicole Crowder, *Washington Post*, 16 November 2014. washingtonpost.com/news/in-sight/wp/2014/10/16/2538/. Accessed 16 October 2023.

53 "Why They Left." Faraz, Sanei, *Human Rights Watch*, 13 December 2012. hrw.org/report/2012/12/13/why-they-left/stories-iranian-activists-exile. Accessed 11 April 2023.

54 "UNHCR - Refugee Statistics." *UNHCR*, www.unhcr.org/refugee-statistics/download/?url=2bxU2f. Accessed 16 October 2023.

55 "Report on 200 Days of Protest Repression/List of at Risk Protesters." *Iran Human Rights*, 4 April 2023, iranhr.net/en/articles/5795/. Accessed 5 April 2023.

56 "Bu ne tesadüf." Kezban Bülbül, *Yeni Şafak*, 9 June 2013. yenisafak.com/gundem/bu-ne-tesaduf-530647. Accessed 11 April 2023.

57 "Purge in Turkey intensifies brain drain." Selin Bucak, *Financial Times*, 28 September 2016, ft.com/content/e7142eb6-7e90-11e6-8e50-8ec15fb462f4. Accessed 11 April 2023.

58 "Growing number of Turkish citizens apply for asylum in Germany." Christina Goßner, *Euractiv*, 8 May 2020. euractiv.com/section/justice-home-affairs/news/an-increasing-number-of-turkish-citizens-apply-for-asylum-in-germany/.

Accessed 16 October 2023.

59   "Germany: Dramatic increase in number of Turkish ref-
      ugees." Elmas Topcu, *DW*, 11 November 2022. dw.com/
      en/germany-dramatic-increase-in-number-of-turkish-refu-
      gees/a-63719538. Accessed 16 October 2023.

60   "Some 32,000 Turkish citizens have entered the US through
      Mexico since 2020." *Stockholm Center for Freedom*, 23 January
      2023. stockholmcf.org/about-32-thousand-turkish-citizens-
      fled-to-u-s-from-mexico-since-2020/. Accessed 11 April
      2023.

61   "Turkey: "Dark day for online free expression" as new 'disin-
      formation law' is passed." *Amnesty International*, 13 October
      2022. amnesty.org/en/latest/news/2022/10/turkey-dark-day-
      for-online-free-expression-as-new-disinformation-law-is-
      passed/. Accessed 16 October 2023.

62   "Turkey 'moves up' to third place in first-time asylum applica-
      tions to EU in 2022." *Duvar English*, 6 July 2023. duvaren-
      glish.com/turkey-moves-up-to-third-place-in-first-time-asy-
      lum-applications-to-eu-in-2022-news-62682. Accessed 11
      July 2023.

63   "UNHCR - Refugee Statistics." *UNHCR*, www.unhcr.org/
      refugee-statistics/download/?url=2bxU2f.

64   "Asylum applications remain at high levels in January" *Euro-
      pean Union Agency for Asylum*, 23 March 2023. euaa.europa.
      eu/news-events/asylum-applications-remain-high-levels-janu-
      ary. Accessed 11 July 2023.

65   "Afghan citizens resettlement scheme." *GOV.UK*, 18 August
      2021. gov.uk/guidance/afghan-citizens-resettlement-scheme.
      Accessed 16 October 2023.

66   "Only 22 Afghans resettled in UK under 'pathway' to help
      vulnerable refugees." Rajeev Syal, *The Guardian*, 23 February
      2023. theguardian.com/uk-news/2023/feb/23/only-22-
      afghans-resettled-in-uk-scheme-vulnerable-refugees-small-
      boats-channel. Accessed 16 October 2023.

67   "Entering the UK to claim asylum." *Right to Remain*, 10

December 2020, righttoremain.org.uk/toolkit/enter-uk-asylum/. Accessed 16 October 2023.

68 "Irregular migration to the UK, year ending December 2022." *GOV.UK*, 23 February 2023. gov.uk/government/statistics/irregular-migration-to-the-uk-year-ending-december-2022/. Accessed 28 March 2023.

69 "Majority of people on small boats crossing Channel last year are refugees, new analysis shows." Lea Corban, *Refugee Council*, 31 January 2023. refugeecouncil.org.uk/latest/news/majority-of-people-on-small-boats-crossing-channel-last-year-are-refugees-new-analysis-shows/. Accessed 16 October 2023.

70 Ibid.

71 "Ukraine's ombudswoman says 400 missing in town of Hostomel." *Reuters*, 6 April 2022. reuters.com/world/europe/ukraines-ombudswoman-says-400-missing-town-hostomel-2022-04-06/. Accessed 11 April 2023.

72 "Ukraine - 2021 Plan Summary." Global Focus, *UNHCR*, 2021. reporting.unhcr.org/ukraine-2021-plan-summary. Accessed 11 July 2023.

73 "UNHCR: One year after the Russian invasion, insecurity clouds return intentions of displaced Ukrainians." *UNHCR*, 23 February 2023. unhcr.org/news/unhcr-one-year-after-russian-invasion-insecurity-clouds-return-intentions-displaced-ukrainians. Accessed 11 July 2023.

74 Ibid.

75 "Russia passes law banning 'LGBT propaganda' among adults." Pjotr Sauer, *The Guardian*, 24 November 2022. theguardian.com/world/2022/nov/24/russia-passes-law-banning-lgbt-propaganda-adults. Accessed 16 October 2023.

76 "Informe CEAR 2023." *CEAR*, cear.es/informe-cear-2023/. Accessed 29 August 2023.

77 "CEAR denuncia las graves dificultades para acceder al asilo en España." María Sevillano, *CEAR*, 19 June 2023. cear.es/cear-denuncia-las-graves-dificultades-para-acceder-al-asilo-en-espana/. Accessed 29 August 2023.

78   Ibid.

79   "Spanish public opinion on immigration and the effect of VOX." Carmen Gonzalez Enriquez, Sebastian Rinken, *Real Instituto Elcano*, 15 April 2021. realinstitutoelcano.org/en/analyses/spanish-public-opinion-on-immigration-and-the-effect-of-vox/. Accessed 16 October 2023.

80   "Artists in Exile: A Conversation with Judith Depaule - We Are Europe." David Bola, *We Are Europe*, 25 May 2022. weare-europe.eu/artists-in-exile-a-conversation-with-judith-depaule/. Accessed 28 March 2023.

81   Lijtmaer, Ruth M. "Social Trauma, Nostalgia and Mourning in the Immigration Experience." American journal of psychoanalysis vol. 82,2 (2022): 305-319. doi:10.1057/s11231-022-09357-8 Accessed 28 Mar. 2023.

82   Ibid.

83   Horst, Cindy, and Katarzyna Grabska. "Introduction: Flight and Exile—Uncertainty in the Context of Conflict-Induced Displacement". Social Analysis 59.1 (2015): 1-18. doi.org/10.3167/sa.2015.590101. Web. Accessed 16 October 2023.

84   Ibid, "Social Trauma, Nostalgia and Mourning in the Immigration Experience."

85   Durak, Mithat & Senol Durak, Emre & Sakiroglu, Mehmet. (2019). The Psychological Effects Of The Losses In Exile Experiences: A Qualitative Research. 579-585. 10.21733/ibadjournal.590318.

86   Ibid.

87   "The Worst Effects of Online Death Threats Are Things No One Can See." Philip Eil, *Vice*, 22 July 2019. vice.com/en/article/qv7yyq/the-worst-effects-of-online-death-threats-are-things-no-one-can-see. Accessed 16 October 2023.

88   "Global Trends Report 2021." *UNHCR*, 2021. unhcr.org/62a9d1494/global-trends-report-2021. Accessed 16 October 2023.

89   Ibid.

90   Ibid.
91   "UNHCR: Global displacement hits another record, capping decade-long rising trend." *UNHCR*, 16 June 2022. unhcr.org/neu/81545-unhcr-global-displacement-hits-another-record-capping-decade-long-rising-trend.html. Accessed 16 October 2023.
92   Malpass, David. Remarks by World Bank Group President David Malpass at Fragility Forum 2022. 7 Mar. 2022, doi.org/10.1596/37773. Accessed 13 July 2023.
93   "Latest Asylum Trends." *European Union Agency for Asylum*, January 2023. euaa.europa.eu/latest-asylum-trends-asylum. Accessed 16 October 2023.
94   Ibid.
95   "DEATHS DURING MIGRATION RECORDED SINCE 2014, BY REGION OF INCIDENT." *Missing Migrants Project*, missingmigrants.iom.int/data. Accessed 16 October 2023.
96   Ibid.

About the Author

Selin is a Turkish-British freelance journalist, currently based in Paris. Born in the UK, she grew up in Turkey and has previously lived in New York and London, where she received a master's in Near and Middle East Studies from SOAS. Previously she was the editor of *Private Equity News* at Dow Jones, and news editor of specialist B2B publication *Citywire Wealth Manager*. She writes about a variety of topics from finance and sustainability to gender diversity and human rights issues in Turkey. She also runs a weekly newsletter for women who want to learn more about finance and economics.

About the Inklings series

This book is part of 404 Ink's Inkling series which presents big ideas in pocket-sized books.

They are all available at 404ink.com/shop.

If you enjoyed this book, you may also enjoy these titles in the series:

Electric Dreams – Heather Parry

Electric Dreams picks apart the forces that posit sex robots as either the solution to our problems or a real threat to human safety, and looks at what's being pushed aside for us to obsess about something that will never happen.

No Dice – Nathan Charles

Risk is embedded in almost every corner of the popular culture we consume; its hidden exposure is a new version of disaster capitalism.

No Dice explores the messy world of gambling, addiction and risk that we encounter daily, from childhood through adulthood, to ask – is it worth the risk? And more so, do we even know what risks we're taking?

No Man's Land – Anne East

Many individuals – especially of non-white heritage – are suspended in an identity limbo. The need to divide and separate our lives, even ourselves, into neat boxes means that many British-born people with no ties to their parental culture are left adrift within our society. This is Anne East's experience.